M000025361

MARINE AIRPOWER

Real Heroes, Volume III

By Randy Jolly

MARINE AIRPOWER

A Tribute To the AirCombat Element
of the United States Marine Corps

by Randy Jolly

TABLE OF CONTENTS

International Standard Book Number 1-885347-02-2

Library of Congress Number 97-072880

© All photos copyright Randy Jolly 1997

except for the following:

Pages 12,13   Capt. Brian J. Bracken

Pages 36,38,39   Lt.Col. J.A. Papay, Jr.

Page 81   Renee Francillion

Published by: Aero Graphics Inc.

4729 Lawler Road - Garland, Texas 75042-4506

(972) 276 2544 FAX (972) 276 5494

Art Production - Active Media, Portland, OR

Printing in Hong Kong through Bookbuilders, Ltd.

All rights reserved. No part of this work may be reproduced or used in any form by any means - graphic, electronic, or mechanical, including photocopying, recording, taping, scanning or any information storage and retrieval system - without the written permission of the publisher

O n May 22, 1912, First Lieutenant Alfred Cunningham reported for flight training duty at Annapolis. By doing so, he became the first Marine aviator and that day in May has since been recognized as the official birthday of Marine Corps aviation.

In the ensuing 85 years the Air Combat Element (ACE) of the Marine Corps has developed into a hard hitting force with awesome capabilities.

Who can help but be inspired by such a proud heritage? Midway, Guadalcanal, Bouganville, Iwo Jima, Okinawa, Kimpo, Chu Lai, Da Nang, and King Abdul Aziz recall to mind epic struggles of mythic dimension.

To name the types of aircraft flown by the Marine Corps over the years is to recite the evolution of military aviation; Curtis C-3, DH-4, Wildcat, Hellcat, Dauntless, Corsair, Panther, Fury, Huey, Cobra, Sea Horse, Sea Knight, Sea Stallion, Skyraider, Crusader, Skyhawk, Intruder and Phantom.

But the aircraft flown and the air battles fought have no meaning unless you take into consideration the human element. It is, after all, the valor, sense of duty and sacrifice of individual Marines who have built the Corps into what it is today. Whether Medal of Honor recipients or anonymous officers and enlisted Marines, it is the personal commitment that has defined the Marine Corps over the years.

By nature, the Marine Corps is expeditionary. It operates on the theory of maneuver combat. Hit hard. Hit Fast. And hit decisively. The ability to move quickly, whether from land bases or from aboard ships at sea, allows the Marines to accomplish their primary mission -- to find the enemy, make contact and destroy him.

Augmenting that mission today, however, is the added burden of responding to the pleas for assistance from embassies and civilians in distress overseas. Evacuating U.S. diplomats and their dependents from areas of escalating tension has become an all too frequent occurrence. The responsibility of protecting and providing relief for populations devastated by famine and despotism has also fallen to the Marines.

It is true that every Marine is a rifleman at heart. And when it comes to protecting and providing support for that dearest of Marine assets, Marine aviators command the respect of their peers for going into harm's way to support their comrades on the ground.

The perspectives of a Marine aviator's life cannot easily be shown in a few hundred photographs. Many of the sorties flown are at night, down low or in terrible weather. As you view the photographs on the following pages just imagine the same scene taking place at night, lights out.

Or, consider a mass assault on a landing zone by a half dozen CH-46s and CH-53s with assault support from two sections of AH-1s. The camera simply cannot photograph the dynamics of such an effort. With dust flying, machine guns blazing and Marines pouring off the ramps, it is an experience that dozens of cameras would fail to capture.

The exhilaration and sheer terror of screaming along at tree top level in the back seat of an F/A-18D can neither be photographed nor adequately described. Especially when the pilot does a "Marine pop," going nose high, inverts and points the nose at the ground, rolls wings level, drops bombs and yanks the aircraft skyward again.

On the following pages are vignettes, snap shots really, of what the Air Combat Element does everyday. When not in actual combat, Marines are busy honing their skills as part of the fully integrated Marine Air Ground Task Force; one of the most powerful and elite forces in the world.

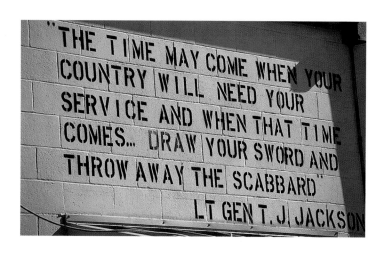

"THE TIME MAY COME WHEN YOUR COUNTRY WILL NEED YOUR SERVICE AND WHEN THAT TIME COMES... DRAW YOUR SWORD AND THROW AWAY THE SCABBARD"

LT GEN T. J. JACKSON

The F/A-18 Hornet gives the Marine Corps an all-weather fighter and attack aircraft that can perform a multitude of missions uniquely suited to the Marine Corps' maneuver combat style. Operating from either land-based airfields, expeditionary airfields or from carrier decks augmenting Carrier Air Wings, the combat proven Hornet gives the Marines the flexibility and firepower to accomplish the central task of every Marine aviator — support of the Marine rifleman. From Westpac to the Persian Gulf to the skies over Bosnia, Marine pilots have flown their Hornets in harm's way with telling results showing they are force to be reckoned with.

The Marine Corps' F/A-18 operations onboard the carrier are the same as the Navy. In actuality, while deployed aboard the carrier, the squadron belongs to the Navy and is at its disposal just like Navy squadrons. The only difference is that when the Marines return home they are still operationally in the Carrier Air Wing but conduct their own training. While embarked with the carrier air wing, the Marine squadrons do a great deal of integrated training with both carrier and non-carrier squadrons.

Prior to embarking on the carrier, the Marines spend an entire month flying once or twice a day doing Field Carrier Landing Practice in preparation for qualifications at the ship. At the carrier, Marine pilots are required to make ten day passes and six night passes at the ship. While the day passes are not new to any Navy or Marine F/A-18 pilots, the night passes are usually the first time a Marine pilot has landed on the ship at night.

It's the world's most **flexible** strike fighter.

Air to air, air to ground. **Day** or night.

The mission is: Protect the **peace.**

Who will **fly** that **mission** with them**?**

McDonnell Douglas **will.**

MCDONNELL DOUGLAS

McDonnell Douglas is proud to build the F/A-18, the world's most advanced strike fighter.

©1996 McDonnell Douglas Corporation

PROUD TO PROTECT THE F/A-18C/D WITH THE AN/ALQ-165 ASPJ

ITT Defense & Electronics

ITT Avionics, 100 Kingsland Road, Clifton, NJ 07014

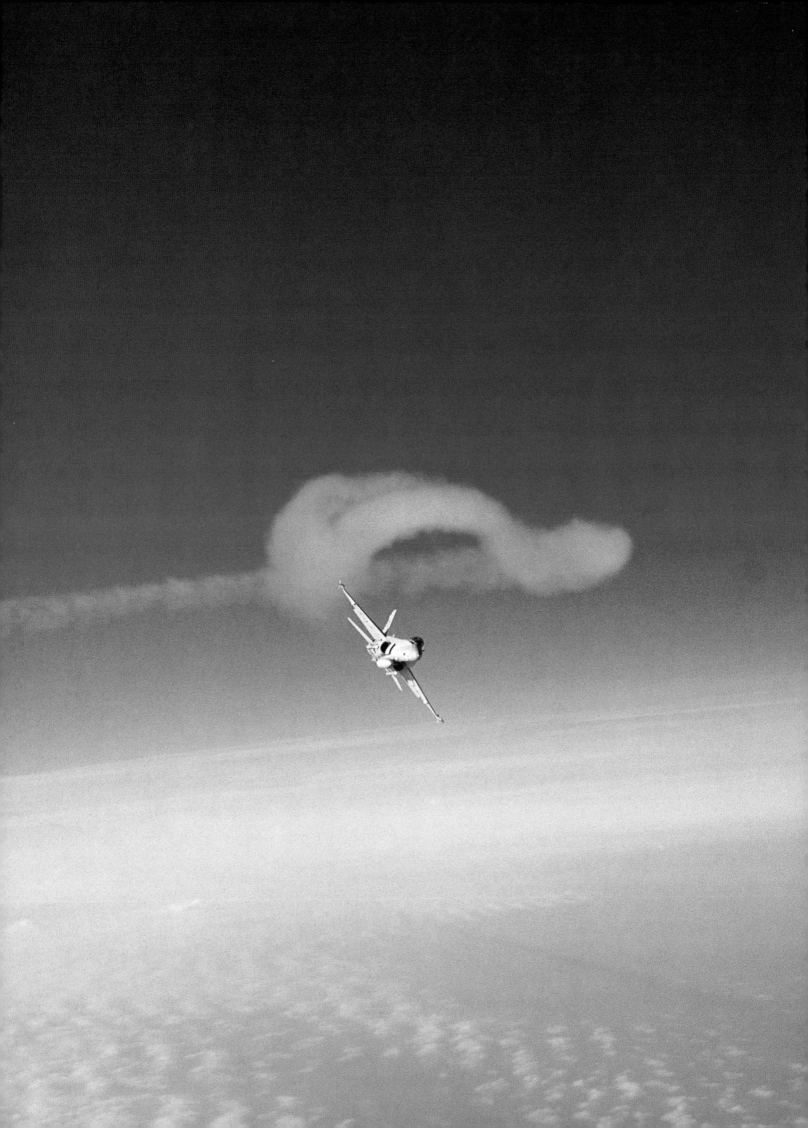

The F/A-18D Night Strike Hornets have enhanced performance engines, upgraded radar and NVG-compatible cockpits. The big difference is the two-man crew. Earlier two-seat F/A-18s were really single-seat airplanes, mission-wise. The F/A-18D is built around the two-man team that drastically decreases individual workload while increasing overall situational awareness.

The pilot flies the aircraft, employs the weapons and assists in operating the sensors. The WSO is the primary operator of the sensors, radar and FLIR. The pilot can focus more attention on flying the aircraft to weapons release while the WSO is working the systems to designate the target. Two brains, four eyes and two bags of situational awareness can be a lifesaver.

Although changes in other systems have boosted the F/A-18D's capabilities, changes in the cockpit have made it a true two-man jet. This team approach allows a division of labor crucial to surviving in the demanding night-attack role, and it enhances mission effectiveness in any other role. The front "office" incorporates multifunction displays (MFDs) that overlay color symbols on mono-chrome sensor presentations. The back cockpit is entirely new. The stick and throttle have been removed, two side-stick displays put in and three MFDs occupy most of the instrument panel. These are identical to the ones in the front cockpit so that the pilot can see everything the Weapons System Officer (WSO) can see and vice versa. This allows tasks to be shared, resulting in greater combat effectiveness.

Since all the displays and cockpit lighting are Night Vision Goggle compatible, the crew can "see" at night by relying either on NVGs or FLIR. The ability to see at night gives the F/A-18D crew the ability to operate around the clock in all kinds of weather and bring a tremendous amount of firepower to bear on a wide range of targets.

The Maverick missile comes in two variants; the LASER Maverick (LMAV) and the IR Maverick (IMAV). Both missiles are designed to penetrate armor, concrete or reinforced bunker type targets.

The IMAV uses infra-red energy to guide to its target. The pilot uses a cockpit display to slew the seeker head onto a target with sufficient contrast to the surrounding background. The pilot then commands lock-on whereby the missile achieves a self track. The pilot can then launch the missile and leave, making the IMAV a true launch and leave, stand off weapon. The IMAV was proven in combat in the Gulf War where the missile was employed with astounding success.

The LMAV uses laser energy to guide to its target. If the launch aircraft is also providing the laser energy, the aircraft can continue to preserve standoff range from the target until missile impact. If the laser energy is provided from another source, the pilot can then launch the missile and leave. The LMAV was proven in combat in Bosnia during the famous Udbina Airfield Strike in November, 1994.

The F/A-18 is equipped with the M61A-1 20mm cannon capable of firing up to 6000 rounds per minute in either the air-to-air or air-to-ground modes. The Hornet carries up to 578 high explosive rounds that explode upon impact.

In air-to-ground mode, the pilot can select the gun either as a stand alone weapon or fire the gun and drop bombs simultaneously. The extreme accuracy of the gun has been proven in combat in both the Gulf War and Bosnia. Strafing runs may be conducted against a wide range of targets from tanks and vehicles to troop formations. The

combination of high explosive rounds, extreme accuracy and high rate of fire make the 20mm cannon a deadly air-to-ground weapon.

In the dynamic world of air combat, the M61A-1 is without question one of the finest air-to-air guns in the world. The F/A-18's radar and on board computers use target aircraft position, range and velocity to present a highly accurate gun solution on the heads up display (HUD) so that the pilot can maneuver his aircraft to place the gun reticle on his opponent and deliver the F/A-18s deadly sting.

The F/A-18 can deliver a multitude of precision guided munitions (PGMs) and non-precision weapons. These weapons can be delivered from a variety of altitudes and dive angles.

For precision guided munitions, the F/A-18 aircrew may choose to use an altitude sanctuary to avoid being exposed to small arms, anti-aircraft artillery and shoulder fired missiles. The crew will initially find the target on radar from as far away as 40nm. As the aircraft approaches the target, the Forward Looking Infrared (FLIR) pod may be used to more accurately designate the target. Finally, the Hornet aircrew can illuminate the target with laser energy, allowing the munitions to guide to the target until impact.

"Hack."
"Iron on target, 30 seconds."

AGM-65 MAVERICK

Maverick Program: 520-663-7445
http://www.hughesmissiles.com

The F/A-18D Night Strike Fighter made its combat debut in the skies over Kuwait during Operation Desert Storm. They were used solely in the Tactical Air Coordinator (Airborne) and Forward Air Control (Airborne) roles. They flew into target areas ahead of strike aircraft, located and identified targets for Coalition aircraft and provided threat updates for as many as 20 strike-fighters in a single 30-minute period.

The Marine F/A-18Ds have continued to rack up impressive accomplishments in Operation Deny Flight (subsequently redesignated Deliberate Guard). As the photos on these two pages attest (taken in the skies over Bosnia), the F/A-18D is employed in the unique "swing role." They are armed and ready to carry out Close Air Support, Offensive Counter Air, Forward Air Controller (Airborne), Suppression of Enemy Air Defenses (SEAD) and Combat Search and Rescue at any time. They could be tasked to any mission any time they are in country.

In November, 1994, there were flight activities out of Udbina Airfield in Croatia that resulted in bombs being dropped in Northern Bosnia. In answer, NATO launched the largest airstrike ever assembled by NATO forces on November 21, 1994. It consisted of over 60 aircraft from NATO. Part of the strike package included Marine F/A-18Ds which were credited with taking out SAM launchers with HARM and LGBs.

Because of the F/A-18D's multi-role capability, it can be tasked for an air to ground mission even if it launched as an air to air sortie. An F/A-18D four-ship formation flying over Bosnia carries a total of four Mk-82 500-pound bombs, two Laser-Guided bombs (LGBs), two four-shot Zuni rocket pods, two High-Speed Anti-Radiation Missiles (HARMs), two AGM-65 Mavericks, two AIM-7s (or AIM-120 AMRAAMs) and eight AIM-9s along with 2,304 rounds of 20mm.

Night Strike Hornet crews have proven the worth of the F/A-18D time and time again through their quick and lethal response — day or night and in all kinds of weather.

For non-precision munitions, a wide variety of delivery modes are available. The aircrew may choose a low altitude ingress to avoid being spotted by enemy radar by taking advantage of man-made and natural terrain features to help navigate to the target. When approaching the target, the Hornet will perform a "pop" maneuver, increasing altitude in order to allow the aircrew to visually acquire the target. The pilot will then roll inverted and pull the Hornet's nose to the target, rolling upright once again to deliver the ordnance from a variety of altitudes and dive angles. The weapons delivery computer on the F/A-18D is so sophisticated that it even corrects for the Earth's rotation ensuring incredible accuracy — even with "dumb" bombs.

VMFAT-101 is one of three F/A-18 Fleet Replacement Squadrons (FRS) more readily known as a "RAG." VMFAT-101 "Sharp-shooters" is the only Marine RAG and trains both pilots and Weapon System Officers and with over 40 aircraft is the largest F/A-18 squadron in the Marine Corps.

The instructor pilots are the core of the squadron. Having completed at least one full fleet tour in the F/A-18 they must be Division Leaders (qualified to lead a 4-ship of Hornets) as well as ACTI's (air combat tactics instructors) Both of these qualifications are earned during the fleet tour. Most instructor pilots have flown at least 1000 hours in the Hornet. Having served in the fleet and completed overseas deployments (some on carriers, some in Westpac, some in Bosnia) instructors take a keen interest in providing the fleet with qualified and prepared aircrew.

All the syllabus training at -101 is geared toward preparing new pilots and WSOs for an operational, combat-ready squadron. As a testament of the training provided, several pilots and WSOs that served in Desert Shield/Desert Storm deployed to the Gulf within months of finishing at the RAG.

Every lecture and flight brief given includes at length discussions on how training, maneuver, and knowledge will serve to benefit the aviator once he gets to the fleet. Being an instructor requires patience, dedication, expertise and a savvy based on experience — knowing when to give a guy a good kick in the butt and when to give him a pat on the back.

There are several phases of training that take place at the RAG. The student starts with the transition phase which includes the basics of flying the Hornet. In the radar intercept phase, the student learns how to operate the radar, flies intercepts and employs weapons beyond visual range.

The next phase, basic fighter maneuver, teaches the student how to fight the jet in the visual arena. In the fighter weapons phase of training the "new guy" integrates the lessons of both the radar intercept and the basic fighter maneuver in order to employ the Hornet in the full combat arena. Intercepts, weapons employment and fighting in the visual arena are brought together and perfected. In the strike phase, the basics of low altitude tactics, bombing and strafing are introduced. Carrier qualifications are the final phase and upon successful completion the pilot or WSO are ready to join an operational squadron.

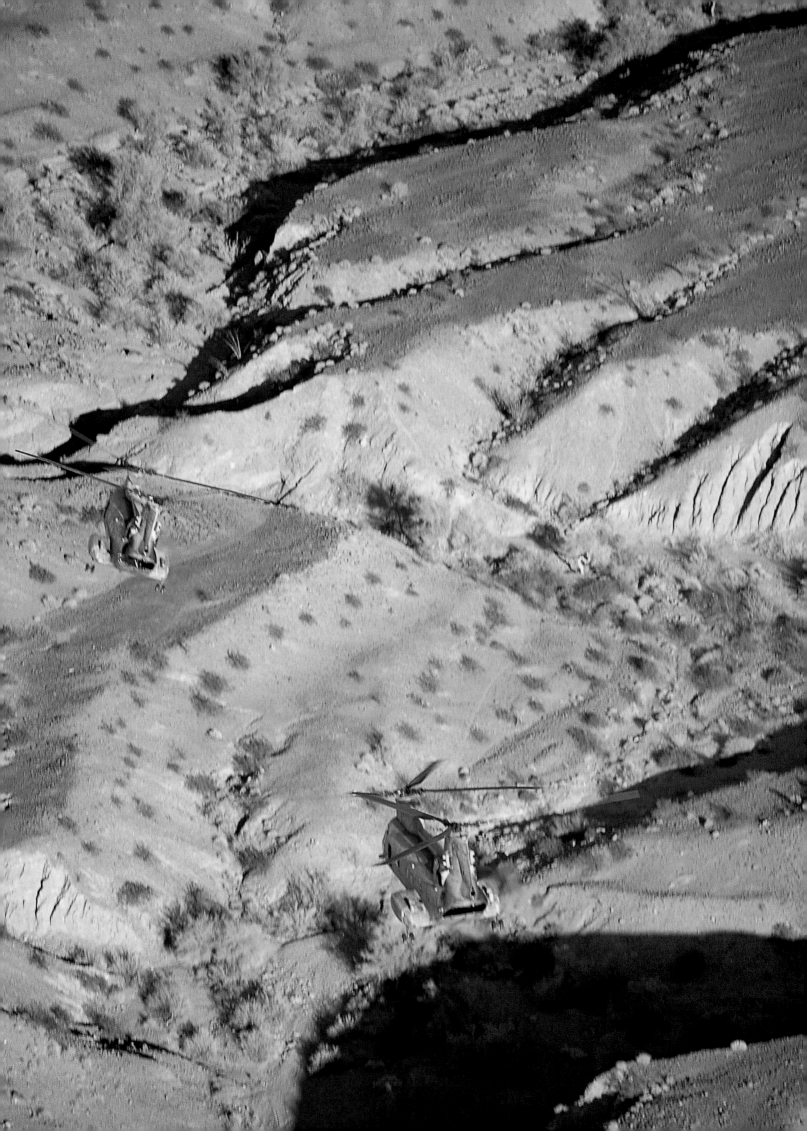

The CH-46E Sea Stallion, or "Phrog" as its known by its crews, is the most numerous type of helicopter in the Marine Corps inventory. Although it has been in continuous service for almost 30 years, the venerable Phrog is the mainstay of the Marine's combat assault capability. Numerous upgrades, modifications and refinements such as new engines, lighter and more durable fiber glass rotors and increased navigational aids plus the advent of Night Vision Goggles have lengthened the CH-46s service life well into the next century.

The Phrog has proven to be one of those pleasant surprises where an aircraft has far exceeded its manufacturer's expectations and original design.

Whether carrying Marines from ship to shore and to hell and back, or hauling bullets and beans to the fight, the CH-46 forms an integral part of the Air Combat Element (ACE) as it supports the Marine Air Ground Task Force (MAGTF). It's a safe bet that where ever Marines happen to be in the world today, they are getting there, day or night, by way of the CH-46E.

Facing Page: While either pilot can manipulate the controls, one pilot flies while the other navigates, monitors instruments, changes radio frequencies and takes care of other cockpit functions.

This page:(top photo), the Crewchief is the mechanical expert on board and is usually the first to arrive and the last to leave the aircraft. In addition to assisting the pilots, the Crewchief is responsible for the safety of passengers as they get on and off the aircraft. (middle and bottom photos) Typically, two observer/gunners round out the CH-46s crew of five. Shown here is a gunner manning one of the two .50 caliber machine guns carried aboard the helicopter for defensive fire support.

The big trade off with any helicopter is fuel for load carrying capability. Though the -46 was designed to carry 25 Marines and crew, the normal load is 12 to 18 combat loaded Marines and all their gear, two .50 cal machine guns and a crew of five. With full fuel tanks, the Phrog can fly up to 375 nautical miles one way. With 3,000 pounds of fuel (one hour and 50 minutes flying time) and a full load of Marines, the -46 can go 100 nautical miles out and back without refueling and have about 20 minutes of extra fuel for delays and deviation in the route. This range can be increased by carrying fewer Marines or gear and replacing that

saved weight with additional fuel.

To get around the restrictions dictated by fuel considerations, the Marines make use of FARPs (Forward Arming and Refueling Point) where helicopters and vehicles can refuel near the front lines. One version of the FARP is the Rapid Ground Refueling (RGR) evolution carried about by the Marine's KC-130s. The -130s land at a dirt strip or abandoned airfield, deploy their refueling lines and refuel the helos as they land, de-arm and taxi into position to take on fuel with rotors turning. The RGR shortens response time and allows the helos to quickly return to the battle.

Previous Page and these pages: Taking advantages of the terrain and the element of surprise are keys to survivability. The benefits of multi-ship flights assaulting the landing zone are obvious. When all the players arrive at once, the enemy's reaction time is reduced and he can't easily bring his weapons to bear on an LZ full of helicopters. Especially if the mass force includes a half-dozen -46s, a couple each of -53s, Hueys and Cobras — all with guns blazing. By landing in a wave, surprise is achieved and the helos can maintain mutual fire support for the aircraft, the crews and the debarking Marines. From the ground commander's perspective, this type of assault allows him to rapidly build his combat power. The number of aircraft involved in a mission is determined by the mission itself, the enemy strength, troops available, time, terrain, support and logistics.

Whether in mass or landing as a section, helicopter crews have to be prepared to handle brown outs. When assaulting the LZ, the helicopter's rotor wash kicks up a substantial amount of dust making visual contact with the surroundings difficult at best. To minimize the effects of a brown out, a pilot will execute a smooth and controlled final approach, choosing the best place to land. He then works his way through a brown out by maintaining forward airspeed on the aircraft and moving slightly ahead of the forming dust cloud as he approaches the ground. As the dust cloud begins to envelope the helicopter, the pilot lowers his altitude and maintains a smooth, controlled movement to the deck. As the pilot feels his way along toward the deck, the crewchief leans out the crew entry door giving the pilots a constant reading as to altitude and making them aware of any obstacles on the ground. Good crew-coordination and communication are essential to landing the aircraft safely.

One key to survival in the helicopter world is to put a rock between the one being shot at and the one doing the shooting. To this end, one element of the tactical mission training is the TERF (terrain flight) mission. During Vietnam, pilots flew high profiles (out of small arms range) and spiraled into landing zones. With the advent and proliferation of man portable air defense weapons, helicopters can no longer use altitude as a sanctuary during the enroute phase of operations. As a result, TERF tactics were developed. By flying low and using the natural obstacles near the ground, the CH-46 crews can further ensure their survivability.

Maintenance is the key factor, and the maintainers the un-sung heroes, in the Phrog's longevity and reliability in combat. One of the mission requirements of every Marine aviation squadron is to perform organizational level maintenance. As can be imagined, a 30-year old helicopter requires plenty of tender loving care. The crewchiefs and maintenance troops provide this care daily. For a typical flight, the crewchief arrives three hours prior to launch to begin preflighting and conducting daily and turnaround inspections. These inspections are accomplished prior to each flight. On average, one hour of flight time equals 12 hours of maintenance.

The maintenance troops keep the Phrogs at peak operating performance regardless of environmental conditions. Though the -46s often look dirty and grimy on the outside from having to take off and land in a blizzard of dust, they are meticulously maintained.

The use of Night Vision Goggles (NVGs) in the real world allows the Marine Corps to exploit the advantages of night. This is especially important for the CH-46 crews who have to fly close to the ground. Since today's potential enemies have limited to nonexistent night vision capabilities, the cover of darkness allows pilots to evade detection. This translates into greater survivability and significantly improves the chances for a successful completion of the mission. While NVGs do not transform the night into day, they do confer a great advantage to the force that can exploit the night.

While the CH-46 has a great reputation for surviving combat, the use of NVGs and the implementation of night operations substantially enhances the old warbird's chances of living to fight another day.

Training, and real-world crises, aren't limited to ground operations. Though the Phrogs usually end up getting in the dirt eventually as they carry Marines to and from the battlefield, they often operate from onboard any one of the many specially configured LHA/LHD amphibious assault ships. Shown on these pages are members of HMM-261(the "Ragin' Bulls") as they prepare to embark for a week's long training exercise aboard the LHD Kearsarge prior to a cruise to the Mediterranean as part of the 22d Marine Expeditionary Unit (MEU). Marine helicopter squadrons routinely deploy for 180 days at a time aboard ship.

The Marines routinely deploy aboard ships such as the LHD 3 Kearsarge. When helicopter squadrons go to the boat the squadron becomes part of the Marine Expeditionary Unit (MEU) and no longer belong to the parent Marine Air Group. The MEU consists of a Battalion Landing Team, a MEU Service Support Group, an Air Combat Element, and the Command Element (headquarters). The reinforced squadron typically consists of 12 CH-46, four CH-53E, four AH-1W, two UH-1N and six AV-8B aircraft.

CH-46 crews doing what they do best — getting Marines to and from shore and hauling bullets and beans to support them. The flight deck has rightfully been called the most dangerous place in the world to work. It is filled with jet engines, spinning rotors, moving aircraft, Marines loading and unloading and a host of other activities in the relatively confined space of a flight deck.

Obviously, this dynamic environment necessitates a well-coordinated team of deck handlers, maintenance personnel and aircrew in order for operations to be conducted safely and efficiently. From an aircrew perspective, landing on a ship requires precision airwork, superior situational awareness and solid training. Not to mention nerves of steel.

As forward presence around the world diminishes due to budget cuts and the political whims of little countries near the sea shore, U.S. interests are today more likely to be guarded by Marines from offshore, aboard ship. As a result, helicopter crews must train to land, take off and resupply from the pitching and undulating decks of amphibious assault ships and to work flawlessly with other aircraft in the ACE, the Ground Combat Element and the Navy.

Rest assured, when Marines are deployed they will be taken into harm's way by the well trained crews in their CH-46E combat assault helicopters

RUNWAY OPTIONAL.

JOINT STRIKE FIGHTER
The Marines' new JSF will be survivable, agile and supportable, bringing new levels of technology to the unique STOVL mission. Lockheed Martin's innovative JSF propulsion system has already been demonstrated in extensive, near-full scale wind-tunnel and ground testing. By adding the advantage of our stealth and fighter experience, the Marines will get an affordable, high performance strike fighter that can strike from anywhere. http://www.lmtas.com/JAST/

LOCKHEED MARTIN

Close Air Support is the Harrier's primary mission, its "raison d'etre." It is designed to carry a wide variety of ordnance including 500 and 1000 pound bombs, LGBs, cluster bombs, rockets and the 25mm cannon. The Harrier also employs two versions of the AGM-65 Maverick. The AGM-65E is laser guided and requires a laser designator from either ground elements or fixed and rotary wing aircraft. When in range, the pilot fires the missile. The target must be continuously designated with the laser throughout the missile's time of flight or the missile will "go stupid", climb, and coast until gravity inevitably pulls it back to earth.

The IRMAV is a much easier weapon to employ in that it does not require external support. It is a "fire and forget" weapon that homes on an infra-red heat source.

IT'S EVERYTHING YOU'D EXPECT IN A MULTIROLE AIRCRAFT. AND ONE THING YOU WOULDN'T.

The Harrier II Plus. APG-65 radar, beyond visual range capability and the ability to operate day, night and in adverse weather. Everything you'd expect from a world-class multirole aircraft. The one thing you wouldn't expect is STOVL. (Short Take Off Vertical Landing).

MCDONNELL DOUGLAS

 ROLLS ROYCE  BRITISH AEROSPACE   HUGHES AIRCRAFT COMPANY

©1996 McDonnell Douglas Corporation

There are several differences between the AV-8B and the AV-8B II Plus. The primary improvement is the addition of the APG-65 radar (the same radar used in the F/A-18). It is used for "air-to-surface" ordnance delivery, though it is also a very capable "air-to-air" radar. The "air-to-surface" mode allows the pilot to identify radar significant ground and sea targets (moving and stationery) through a reduced visibility environment. Though the II Plus is not currently rated as an "all weather" platform, its ability to operate in reduced visibility increases the aircraft's survivability by

allowing the pilot to identify potential targets while avoiding detection by optical, laser and infra-red guided threats.

As with the "night attack" Harrier, the II Plus is equipped with a full night systems suite which includes a navigation forward looking infra-red (NAVFLIR), ASN-130 ring laser INS, digital moving map, night vision goggles, and a fully NVG compatible lighting package.

With an upgraded engine providing more thrust and improved angle of attack handling and other improvements the II Plus is even more potent and survivable.

Close Air Support, as the name implies, is down and dirty work. The Harrier's agility, quick response time and ability to carry tons of ordnance make it especially suited for such unique work. Operation Desert Storm was a perfect example of how the Harrier can be employed in combat. AV-8's, both land and ship based, flew some of the highest sortie rates of the war. Pilots averaged between 40 and 46 combat missions. A total of 86 Harriers deployed to Southwest Asia by the end of March, 1991. The 60 land based Harriers,

from VMA-231, VMA-311 and VMA-542, flew roughly 3,000 combat sorties. During the 42 days of conflict, 86 aircraft flew a total of 3,383 combat sorties and delivered 5.95 million pounds of ordnance against Iraqi forces.

Essentially, whenever the Marines are involved, the Harriers are there. VMA-223, while sailing with the 24th Marine Expeditionary Unit aboard the USS Nassau, participated in missions over Bosnia. Harriers also supplied helo escort support for Capt. O'Grady's rescue.

VMAT-203 is the only Fleet Replacement Squadron (better known as the "RAG") for the Harrier community. It also trains the Spanish and Italian pilots.

A new pilot can expect to spend six months at the RAG, flying nominally 95 flight hours and 60 or so simulator hours. While at the squadron, the new pilot will go through familiarization, instruments, navigation, air-to-ground weapons using systems, various tactical applications, basic air combat maneuvering, using nozzles as well as conventional tactics.

The new pilots also get formation flying

(day and night), tactical formation training, mission planning, aerial refueling behind KC-130s, and restricted site operations (landing in the trees on pads, expeditionary field work and field carrier landing practice). In each hop, V/STOL skills and plenty of practice in take-offs and landings are stressed since the new, conventionally minded pilot has to incorporate himself into the V/STOL mentality — nozzles and then power, stop and then land.

It's a busy and demanding schedule. Quite a challenge. But, worth the effort when the end result is being assigned to an operational squadron.

SFW

Sensor Fuzed Weapon

... is available NOW to meet current AND future USMC needs

Power Projection:
Multiple Options Builds More Punch
In The Limited-Size Expeditionary Package

TEXTRON Systems
201 Lowell Street,
Wilmington, MA 01887
TEL (508) 657-1276 ▪ (508) 657-6644

The great thing about the Harrier is that it can operate anywhere close to the action; from expeditionary airfields (shown above) or from the deck of a ship (at right aboard the LHD-3 Kearsarge). Although vertical landing operations aboard ship are really no different from field operations, the fact that the deck is usually pitching and rolling makes it a more daunting task.

Rolling out behind the ship at about a half mile, the pilot pulls the nozzles to the "hover stop." The Harrier is now converting all its thrust to lift as the wing loses its lift and the pilot is required to add a considerable amount of power to keep it level. With no thrust directed aft, the airplane is coasting to a stop alongside the ship. When the pilot sees his landing spot, he checks back on the stick to raise the nose and the airplane stops. A sideways slide over the deck and a moment to stabilize and ensure he's over his landing spot and he descends to the deck. The airplane is landed firmly and the throttle is chopped on touchdown to prevent a bounce. Once on the deck, the Harrier taxies to its parking spot or is positioned for its take-off roll at the forward end of the deck.

CH-53E SUPER STALLION.
ANY MISSION, ANYTIME, ANYPLACE.

Sikorsky
A United Technologies Company

The CH-53E Super Sea Stallion provides the Marine Corps with a tremendous assault support capability. It can move massive amounts of cargo and equipment and people. During the first few waves of an assault, CH-53Es and CH-46s are both called on to quickly build up combat power and, in subsequent waves, the CH-53E carries in Marines as well as external equipment such as light armored vehicles and heavy artillery.

The Super Sea Stallion provides the Assault Commander with a variety of options. With its long range it can go deep into enemy territory. It's speed is compatible with the assault support escort Cobras, and with its lift capability, can recover and retrieve any aircraft and personnel forced down enroute so that no personnel or equipment are left behind.

In the dynamic world of flying combat assault helicopters, crew coordination is an essential element. Not only for the success of the mission but in staying alive. The Helicopter Aircraft Commander (HAC) and the co-pilot fly the aircraft while the crew chief and the gunner/observer take care of things in the back whether the load is Marines or equipment.

Practically every phase of the mission requires the complete coordination and communication between everyone on board. In the aerial refueling evolution, all eyes are outside to find the tanker. Since tanking at night is a "lights out" operation, and the CH-53E crew

is on NVGs, it is incumbent on each crew member to provide information as to where the tanker is in relation to the helicopter and the other helicopters in the flight.

When assaulting the landing zone, the crew chief and gunner/observer provide altitude and drift information to the pilots as they fly the aircraft and deal with the effects of brownouts (in the dirt) or whiteouts (in the snow). During external lift operations, the crewchief gives voice commands to the pilots regarding the hover and coordinates with the helicopter support teams to ensure that loads are properly rigged and stabilized for flight.

The CH-53 is the most combat survivable helicopter in the world. It's speed, long range and maneuverability make it ideal for the high threat TRAP (tactical recovery of allied personnel) mission. Flying with a section of AH-1W Cobras, a section of CH-53s (each with 37 fully combat loaded Marines) can rapidly ingress and egress enemy territory before the enemy has a chance to respond. Shown on these pages are CH-53 Super Sea Stallions conducting suppressing fire with their .50 caliber machine guns on short final during an assault support landing mission. With a section of Cobras providing assault support escort, the CH-53 can enter enemy airspace at 170 knots at 25 feet off the ground and with FLIR and imbedded GPS fly precisely to a location, pick up downed airman (as in the Scott O'Grady rescue) or civilians (as in the recent evacuations in Albania) and be out of hostile territory quickly.

In simple terms, the EA-6B Prowler keeps people alive and gets airplanes to and from the target by putting out the enemy's eyes. The eyes in this case are electronic. Using the ALQ-99 tactical jamming system, a Prowler's crew can fill an air defense radar screen with meaningless fuzz, rendering it totally ineffective. When the enemy's search radars are down, the SAM radars are forced to come on the air to search for targets on their own and that is when the Prowler will fire a HARM anti-radiation missile to kill the site. Additionally, it takes a lot of voice communication to run air defense systems and the Advanced Capability upgrade to the EA-6B adds a communication jammer to attack the air defense network. The Prowlers have proved their worth time and again. In Desert Storm, for instance, Prowler crews took the best air defense system money could buy and brought it to its knees. One reason Coalition aircraft took so few losses is because of the effectiveness of the EA-6B and it crews.

The Prowler carries a crew of four. The pilot, seated up front on the left flies the aircraft and fires the HARM missile. There are three Electronic Warfare Officers (ECMOs) on board. ECMO One, seated in the right front seat, handles all radio control, navigation systems and defensive countermeasure systems as well as the HARM missile controls. In the backseat on the right is ECMO Two and on the left is ECMO Three. The officers sitting in those seats operate the ALQ-99 Tactical Jamming System.

Though the Prowler is admittedly not as fast as the Air Force's EF-111s it can comfortably ingress a target at 480 KIAS (knots indicated air speed) and maxes out around 520 KIAS when fully combat loaded. The EA-6B can be refueled by Air Force and Marine Corps tankers as well as by tankers from other air forces so that it can remain on station for as long as the crew can stand it (normally eight hours).

While the Prowler may be a bit slower than its EF-111 counterpart, it is far superior in the areas of frequency jamming. Another big plus for the Prowler is it ability to launch the HARM and kill the enemy radar site.

We've Trained Every Marine Corps Electronic Warfare Officer Since the 1970's. That's Not Just A Track Record. It's Some Sort Of World Record.

The U.S. military has come to rely on the simulators and testing equipment made by the AAI Corporation. We're proud to have played a part in its success, and look forward to leading the way in electronic warfare technology for years to come.

Jamming enemy radars and blinding an enemy's air defense system is a dangerous business. Prowlers are usually the first in and the last out, plotting the enemy's defense network, reporting it back to the commander and ingressing the target as part of the strike package to jam the enemy radars. The popular idea of sneaking in under the enemy's radar coverage is fine when the combination of terrain and radar location will allow it. But when the opposition has sophisticated air defense systems, like those found in Iran, Iraq and Libya, there simply isn't enough of a gap to exploit. By using the Prowler to blind the radars, strike packages create their own gap to "sneak in."

© 1996 Northrop Grumman Corporation

* Information Warfare

The ability to exploit, deceive and disrupt adversary information systems while simultaneously protecting our own. Example: EA-6B Prowler.

In the future, conflicts will be resolved with information as well as hardware. Northrop Grumman has the capability to create and integrate advanced Information Warfare technologies, such as electronic counter-measures and sensors. Northrop Grumman. Systems integration, defense electronics, military aircraft, precision weapons, commercial and military aerostructures. The right technologies. Right now.

NORTHROP GRUMMAN

The AH-1W Cobra, despite its small size is capable of carrying a wide assortment of armament; the M197 20mm cannon, 2.75" and 5.0" rockets with multiple warhead types, BGM-71 TOW, AGM-114 Hellfire, AIM-9 Sidewinder, AGM-112A Sidearm and more. As a result, it is the ideal Close Air Support asset for Marines on the ground. One of the advantages of employing the Hellfire is that Cobra crews can fire the missile from behind a masking feature without exposing the shooter to hostile fire. It's ability to shoot missiles, rockets and the cannon on the run or from a hover position make the Cobra a key player on the battlefield.

Since the AH-1W Cobra is so heavily armed and highly maneuverable, it gives the Marines the kind of on-call, close in fire support they need in dealing with hostile troops or enemy armor.

Both crew positions in the aircraft are manned by pilots so the flying duties can be handed off, back and forth, between the pilots as they race toward a target. While one pilot flies the aircraft, the other is free to accurately target and fire the weapons. The Cobra can laser designate its own targets or laser designate for other shooters as well.

Shipboard operations require yet a different set of skills from land-based operations. When an aircraft is fully loaded, it will come along side the ship and point its nose out to sea and come aboard side ways. Landing and taking off from a rolling and pitching deck, especially at night, is both mentally and physically demanding. Not only is the horizon often imperceptible, there are very few reference points available and the two-dimensional picture presented by NVGs makes descent and closure difficult.

Fighting Capabilities That Bring Peace Of Mind.

©1996 Bell® Helicopter Textron Inc., all rights reserved.

The Bell AH-1W SuperCobra is the most powerful, most versatile attack helicopter in the world. Deploying the greatest array of weapons you can fly, including HELLFIRE, TOW, SideWinder and Zuni rockets. And all for the lowest acquisition cost of any gunship in production. ◆ No wonder the U.S. Marine Corps and fighting forces throughout the globe rely on the SuperCobra. With the highest power-to-weight ratio of any attack helicopter and a new Night Targeting System, it can fulfill any attack mission requirement. Even under adverse weather, saltwater and desert conditions that would ground lesser aircraft. In fact, statistics from Desert Storm show that the SuperCobra's reliability and 92% mission readiness rate were superior to all other attack helicopters by as much as 24%. ◆ And, just like every Bell you can buy, the SuperCobra has the lowest life-cycle and maintenance costs in its class. To find out more, contact your Bell Helicopter representative today.

Bell Helicopter
TEXTRON
A Subsidiary of Textron Inc.

P.O. Box 482 ◆ Ft. Worth, TX 76101 ◆ FAX (817) 280-3631 ◆ Call 1-800-FLY-BELL (1-800-359-2355).

The KC-130 is one of the unsung heroes of the Air Combat Element. Its multimission capabilities include in-flight refueling, aerial delivery of personnel and cargo, Medivac, rapid ground refueling, airborne direct air support, search and rescue and a host of other duties. Somehow, the sobriquet of "trash haulers" does not adequately convey the valuable contributions made by KC-130 crews in support of the MAGTF's fast-paced maneuver combat.

With its long range and cargo carrying capacity, the KC-130 can transport and support Marines anywhere in the world. The crews of Marine Hercs work together as a team to expand the reach and impact of the strike forces on the ground or in the air. Typically, a crew consists of two pilots, a navigator, flight engineer, one or two load-masters and a flight mechanic. Operating from austere forward locations as well as land bases far removed from the area of conflict, KC-130 crews and their aircraft provide the vital link of ensuring that logistical support flows smoothly and uninterrupted.

The new KC-130J makes rapid ground refueling more rapid.

It may look like the tanker you've come to rely on over the years. But the new KC-130J Hercules Tanker is packed with an amazing array of high-technology -- improvements that help the aircraft to fly higher, farther, faster and less expensively than ever.

We have automated the fuel system and simplified fuel management tasks. We've fully integrated a digital avionics architecture and provided a state-of-the-art flight station and propulsion system. This allows the KC-130J to increase refueling speed by 30 knots and to operate with improved economy, resulting in greater fuel give.

We've done all this for one reason only. To help you achieve the goals of your mission. It's been our *modus operandi* since the Hercules debuted in 1955. And with this all-new, cost-efficient aircraft, it will continue to be for years to come.

LOCKHEED MARTIN

Mission Success

http://www.lmco.com/

LOCKHEED MARTIN

Mission Success

http://www.lmco.com/

The Rapid Ground Refueling evolution provides fuel to other aircraft or tanks and vehicles that operate on jet fuel at austere locations where no other source of fuel is readily available. The KC-130, with its large fuel capacity and its ability to land at unimproved sites, gives other Marine assets greater range and flexibility. The RGR site can be anywhere the KC-130 can land: military or civilian airfields, minimum operating strips such as bomb-damaged airfields, taxiways on airfields, sections of highway or roadways. Anywhere there is a 5000' x 50' section of level ground, the KC-130 can land, set out its refueling lines and begin refueling thus providing fuel to the forward edge of the battle area and increasing the range of tanks and armored vehicles as well as helicopters and other aircraft.

On a typical wartime RGR sortie, the KC-130 would depart from a secure airfield with 65,000 pounds of fuel and fly for two hours to the RGR site 500 miles away. After landing and rolling out the refueling hoses, the -130 could remain on station for an hour with 30,000 to 35,000 pounds of fuel to give away to tanks, vehicles or aircraft such as AV-8Bs, CH-53s, UH-1s, AH-1Ws and CH-46s.

With its hoses deployed and the RGR operation set up, aircraft to be refueled land, de-arm, deplane any passengers and taxi to the refueling area. After they refuel, they taxi to the staging area where they re-arm and board any passengers and press on with their mission.

Because RGR sites are normally temporary facilities, transitory in nature and established for specific durations and mission, the ultimate objective is to minimize response time and decrease turnaround time in support of sustained operations. To this end, the KC-130s and their crews are ideally suited, bringing in fuel to remote areas, spending as little time on the ground as possible and departing the area as soon as the RGR evolution is completed.

The Marines employ their KC-130s to support both fixed wing aircraft and helicopters in the air refueling role. Depending on the scenario, the rendezvous for the refueling mission is usually performed with with the KC-130 flying a racetrack pattern, anchored at a point over the ground or the water or enroute to a selected destination. With the KC-130 anchored, the crew plans to roll out on the outbound heading from the anchor point at a predetermined time, or simply flies the racetrack pattern and waits for the receivers to arrive during a given time frame. Enroute tanking is usually performed in order to get the receivers to a selected destination. The KC-130 crew plan to arrive at a specified point at a specified time and the receivers plan to meet the tanker there, then continue ahead after aerial refueling.

The entire aerial refueling operation can be conducted in complete radio silence as long as the mission is thoroughly briefed. Fixed wing aerial refueling is usually flown from 15,000 to 25,000 feet but can be flown as low as 500 feet at speeds ranging from 215 to 250 knots.

While jets rendezvous on the tanker, the tanker will join on helicopters below 5,000 feet and at speeds from 110 to 120 knots to complete helicopter aerial refueling.

Aerial refueling is performed day or night. The big consideration, of course, is visibility. Helicopter crews almost always use Night Vision Goggles (NVGs) during the aerial refueling evolution, necessitating them turning off most of their exterior lights. With lights out and flying in the dark, it makes putting eye-balls on helos a difficult task at best since the KC-130s are not NVG capable. The only visual reference for the tanker crew is the upper rotating beacon of the last helo in the formation (affording virtually no depth perception). To complicate matters, the tanker is usually heavy with a full load of fuel and flying near their approach speeds (often only 20 knots above stall speed).

With fixed wing aerial refueling the job is much easier at night since the jets use their radars and NVGs to locate and join on the tanker.

By the time the Bell/Boeing V-22 Osprey is operational, the CH-46 will have served the Marine Corps for over 50 years. With the proliferation of precision weapons and an ever growing sophistication of other threats, carrying Marines into battle aboard the venerable -46 will soon be like competing in today's Indy 500 driving a 64 Chevy — regrettably, deadlier.

The V-22's revolutionary tiltrotor technology of taking off and landing like a helicopter yet flying at speeds of an airplane have real-world implications for the battlefield today and will dramatically impact the outcome on the battlefields of tomorrow. With its survivability, unlimited range, 270-knot speed and the ability to carry 24 combat loaded Marines, the V-22 underscores the importance of getting there first with the most. The Osprey will allow commanders the options for flexible and selective engagements which will overwhelm an enemy force quickly and decisively, thus minimizing the exposure of Marines to hostile fire and protecting one of the greatest assets in the world -- American lives.

Whether in peacetime engagements, deterrence and conflict or prevention of hostilities, the inherent mobility and combat capability of the V-22 will assist the Marines to do what they do best --Fight and Win.

HOW MANY MORE REASONS DO WE NEED TO BUILD THE V-22 SOONER INSTEAD OF LATER?

PERSIAN GULF, 1990-1991

SOMALIA, 1993

HAITI, 1993

LIBERIA, 1996

Today's world is volatile. Full of hot spots. The question is not whether American lives will be at risk, but when and where. That's why a long-range, rapid-deployment, survivable combat aircraft is vital to our nation's global interests. And why it's essential to build V-22s sooner instead of later.

The V-22 utilizes its revolutionary tiltrotor technology to combine the speed and range of a fixed-wing turboprop with the vertical takeoff and landing capabilities of a helicopter. This multi-role transport replaces 40-year-old technology.

Increasing the V-22's production rate will not only get the aircraft to the Marines and Special Operations Forces more quickly, our nation could also **save billions** in total program costs. For the sake of our men and women in uniform, as well as the budget, sooner is better. Now is the time for action. To learn more, contact our World Wide Web site.

http://www.boeing.com

BELL BOEING   ALLISON
The V·22 Tiltrotor Team
A JOINT SERVICE PROGRAM

©1996 Bell® Helicopter Textron Inc./Boeing Helicopters.

The UH-1 Huey has been around, in one form or another, since the days of Vietnam. The upgraded and highly modified UH-1N is the jack-of-all-trades helicopter used by the Marine Corps and is employed in a variety of ways; armed escort for assault support operations, airborne control and co-ordination, search and rescue and aeromedical evacuation of casualties from the field.

The H-1 is also an outstanding platform when used in the role of Forward Air Control Airborne (FAC/A). This mission requires considerable concentration and daring on the part of Huey crews as they support Close Air Support aircraft. Using terrain and low level tactics to mask their presence, UH-1N crews locate and identify targets, pass information on to CAS aircraft or artillery and mark the targets while providing accurate situational updates of conditions in the target area as strike aircraft execute their attacks.

The UH-1N has a crew of four: the Helicopter Aircraft Command (HAC), Co-Pilot, and two crew chief/gunners. The flight controls and fire control systems are integrated and interchangeable and either pilot can fly the aircraft. The crew chief/gunners operate and maintain the weapons onboard and assist with landings and takeoffs by providing visual references and ground clearance for the pilots as well as assisting any passengers. They are also responsible for the maintenance and repair of the aircraft before, during and after flight.

Depending on the mission, the UH-1N can carry different configurations of armament including the M-240 7.62 machine-gun, M-60 7.62mm machine-gun, GAU-17A 7.62 Gatling Gun, GAU-16 .50 caliber machine-gun as well as 2.75"

rockets with multiple warhead types.

In the FAC/A role, Huey pilots mark the target with a white phosphorous (WP) rocket and, over a nine-line brief inform the attacking aircraft of the target's precise location.

The Marine Corps' Combined Arms Exercise (CAX) is a program that has evolved over the past decade from a 12-day deployment with a very structured three-day exercise into a 22-day intense training cycle involving a series of progressive live-fire exercises. The objectives of the CAX are to exercise and evaluate active and Reserve Fleet Marine Force units and Marine Air Ground Task Forces (MAGTF) in command, control and coordination of combined arms within a maneuver warfare, live-fire environment.

Since the CAX exercise is the most realistic live-fire training opportunity in the Marine Corps, it is designed to provide commanders the experience of employing all weapons systems of the MAGTF in support of the Marines on the ground. About 2,000 Marines and sailors participate in the event which uses the "building block" approach, starting with small unit training and culminating with a three-day final exercise.

The working and living conditions at Camp Wilson are austere and the operations tempo is accelerated to closely resemble real world conditions as much as possible.

At CAX a detachment or a whole squadron supports a complete Marine Air Ground Team in a battalion sized maneuvering exercise against a constructive enemy force. It provides lots of squadron training with combined arms run just as a real war with lots of live ordnance and practical, high-tempo, heavy workload operations.

It's a good opportunity for Marines to experience how the MAGTF is integrated in the combined arms scenario. Every Marine, no matter what their job, is involved. To maintainers and ordnance troops on the flight line it means hauling bombs and rockets and quickly loading up the aircraft. For "hot pit" crews it means turning aircraft as quickly as possible so the aircrews can re-arm and launch when the action is surging. It means aircrews fly numerous sorties in a single day or night in support of the Ground Combat Element.

The flightline at Camp Wilson, the expeditionary airfield at
29 Palms, gives crewchiefs and maintenance crews a first hand view
of what it will be like in combat. The operations tempo is high with
aircraft landing and taking off all hours of the day and night with
live ordnance. There's no rest for the weary, just like it would be in
a real battle, and the Marines work hard to ensure that the aircraft
are ready to go when the aircrews arrive.

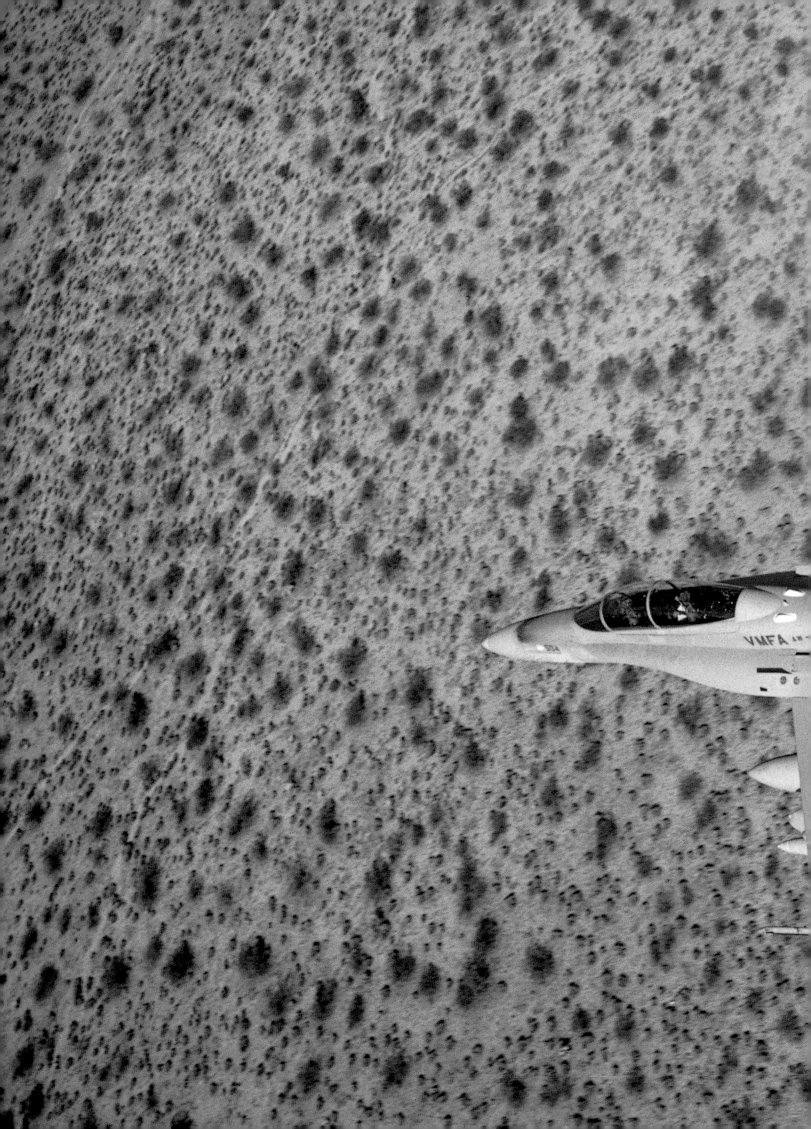

Maintenance doesn't take a vacation when the squadron deploys to CAX. In fact, wherever the squadron deploys they are required to maintain organizational maintenance. Whether its in the heat of the desert, aboard ship or in the freezing cold, the aircraft maintenance must continue apace of operations.

One of the keys to the success of Marine aviation is the consistently high quality of work performed by the crewchiefs and maintenance personnel.

The reality of the matter is that anytime you have high performance aircraft around jet fuel there is the possibility of fire. Aircraft Fire and Rescue Marines frequently train fighting pooled fuel fires using water. The training is designed to build confidence, fire fighting techniques and team-working skills as applied to simulated crash situations.

The temperatures from the radiant heat can reach above 1,000 degrees, requiring Aircraft Firefighters to wear specially designed reflective clothing called Proximity Suits. In addition to the suits, fire fighters use a self-contained breathing apparatus that protects them from the by-products of combustion that would be harmful to their health.

Marine Firefighters always perform their duties in a minimum of two-man teams. In the photo, a back-up man is seen with his hand on the shoulder of a nozzle man. This technique is often used to keep the team in synchronization as they aggressively attack the fire. The hand on the shoulder is an essential form of communication between the two Marines. This technique prevents the possibility of a fire re-flash behind the team.

The "Snipers" of VMFT-401, based at Marine Corps Air Station Yuma, Arizona, are the only adversary squadron in the Marine Corps. Flying F-5 Tiger II aircraft, the Snipers simulate tactics flown by former Soviet counterparts in training Marine squadrons to the potential threats they would face in combat. The great majority of adversarial tactics activity is flown in the Yuma area as other squadrons deploy to the area to take advantage of the training. VMFAT-101, the F/A-18 Fleet Replacement Squadron, deploys to Yuma ten times a year to train with the Snipers and the MAWTS-1 Weapons and Tactics Instructor and Marine Division Tactics courses also take advantage of their expertise.

VMFT-401 takes its show on the road throughout the year visiting other Marine Corps Air Stations and participates frequently in Combined Arms Exercises at 29 Palms, California.

Twice a year (beginning in September and March), Marine Aviation Weapons and Tactics Squadron One (MAWTS-1) conducts a seven week Weapons and Tactics Instructor course. The object of the course is to "train the trainer" and graduate a fully qualified individual who returns to his unit as the primary weapons and tactics educator.

The first half of the course is academics taking the student from generic overview to commonalities of various elements to specific applications of his squadron and aircraft type.

The second half of the course, the Flight Phase, progresses from specific to common to generic. In the first phase, students execute weapons employment and delivery profiles specific to their aircraft type. The second phase shifts to flight evolution's combining aircraft with similar mission profiles. The final phase is the total integration of Marine assets performing the six functions of Marine Aviation (Aerial Reconnaissance, Antiair Warfare, Assault Support, Control of Aircraft and Missiles, Electronic Warfare and Offensive Air Support). The final phase of WTI ends in a FINEX (Final Exercise) that is little short of a small war with all elements of the Marine Air Command and Control System, including ground elements, participating.

At the conclusion of the course, the newly qualified Weapons and Tactics Instructor is ready to return to his parent command and assume the role of unit training manager and tactics instructor. While normally associated with flying squadrons and MACCS units, the remaining WTI graduates will also return to their Marine Wing Communications Squadron or Marine Aviation Logistics Squadron, and intelligence billets, as well as ground combat units to pass on their knowledge of how Marine Aviation integrates into the MAGTF.

The Marines employ two antiaircraft missle systems. The Light Antiaircraft Missile Battalion (LAAM BN) which employs the HAWK missile and the Low Altitude Air Defense Battalion (LAAD BN) which employs the Stinger missile. Shown above is the Avenger which is mounted on the standard HUMMV chassis. The system passively acquires, identifies and provides azimuth location of threat and friendly air targets based on IFF information. The system can engage fixed wing aircraft, helicopters, UAVs and cruise missiles. The system includes eight Stinger missiles and a .50 caliber machine gun and a crew of two.

At right, a two-man Stinger team.

ACKNOWLEDGEMENTS

Without the approval and support of the Commandant, Real Heroes, Volume III, Marine Airpower would never have existed. To General Charles Krulak goes my deepest and heartfelt thanks.

Brigadier General C.L. Stanley and his staff at HQ USMC Public Affairs supported the project from the very beginning and provided unique opportunities to visit and photograph Marines in action. Captain T.V. Johnson shepherded the project from start to finish and, in typical Marine fashion, went "above and beyond" in paving the way for my visits to the various Marine Corps Air Stations.

Major General Mike Ryan and Major General Fred McCorkle enthusiastically opened the doors to their respective commands by signing off on my requests. Moreover, through their outstanding leadership, the squadrons under their command were exceptionally cooperative.

On the operational level, there are so many Marines who deserve mentioning it would take several more pages. In listing individuals who played significant roles in my being at the right place at the right time, surely somebody will be left out. Having stated that, however, the following officers went out of their way to demonstrate by example what Marine aviators do for a living. My thanks to Colonel Jim Amos, Colonel John Castellaw, Colonel James Collins, Colonel Ken Conaster, Colonel Mike Soniak, Lt.Col. Tim Hanifen, Lt.Col. D.C. House, Lt.Col. Douglas Jerothe, Lt.Col. Douglas Lovejoy, Lt.Col. Jack Suter, Lt.Col. Bob Tomon, Lt.Col. J.A. White, Major Conord, Major Kurt Miller, Major W.L. Niblock, Captain R.A. Domingue, Captain David Dowling, Captain Leo Kilgore and Captain Mike Shewfelt.

I am indebted to the enlisted Marines in Life Support and the Crewchiefs out on the flight line. They were always eager to help and showed great patience as I suited up and climbed into their aircraft.

Special thanks, too, to Lt.Col. Rick Muegge, who helped me understand how to endure loss and put sacrifices into perspective.

Another special group of men who deserve recognition are my pilots. They had to interpret my requests and demonstrate superb airmanship while coordinating safe and successful flights: Spanky Benson, Luther Brown, J.C. Burgin, Harry Constant, Bob Cotterell, Randy Ferguson, Chili Hesford, Curly Lambrecht, Chili McFarland, Marty Rollinger, Bugsy Siegal, Jack Snyder and Mike Thumm.

A picture may be worth a thousand words, but Captain John Sherrell made words count for a lot in articulating what it's like to fly.

On the civilian side of the house I'm deeply indebted to Ted Herman, Tim Hill, Jim McClain and Gary Van Gysel who provided guidance, support and proved beyond a shadow of a doubt that "once a Marine...always a Marine."

And, finally, thanks to my dear friend Lt.Col. J.A. Papay. It was his inspiration that brought about this book. One night at 29 Palms as we sat in folding chairs propped up against his tent, he gave me an insight into the world of the Marine aviator. In the fading twilight, as the roar of jet engines and the muffled beating of helicopter blades died to a hush, Joe explained to me the depth of pride and the call to duty each Marine feels. From him I gained an understanding of the *esprit de corps* that sets a Marine apart from everyone else. If Real Heroes, Marine Airpower is successful in conveying that unique bond, then it is to Lt.Col. Papay's credit. If not, I take all the blame.

What is it like working with the Marines of the Air Combat Element? Perhaps the World War II correspondent Ernie Pyle said it best when he wrote, "The ties that grow between men who live savagely together, relentlessly communing with Death, are ties of great strength. There is a sense of fidelity to each other in a little corps of men who have endured."

To one and all, thanks for the memories.

Semper Fi,
Randy Jolly